CLOSE TO MY HEART

A Guided Workbook for Children After a Loved One Dies

Written by **Susan Foley, M.D.**
and **Regen Foley**

Special Thanks to:

and the

Albert E. and Birdie W. Einstein Fund, Inc.

For making publication of this book possible.

© 2009 Susan Foley and Regen Foley

Requests for permission to make copies of any part of this work should be mailed to The Sunshine Project, Inc., 1004 Grand Isle Way, Palm Beach Gardens, FL 33418.

For more information about The Sunshine Project please visit www.SunshineProj.org.

ISBN: 978-1539494713

Library of Congress Control Number: 2009903493

Dedicated to

Rick Sunshine
08/26/56 - 10/05/98

Always close to our hearts

NOTE FOR PARENTS AND OTHER ADULTS WHO CARE

The goal of this book is to help grieving children who are dealing with the death of a loved one. It was written to gently guide children in a positive fashion. It can also aid the child's caretaker in acknowledging and dealing with the child's pain. This is not an easy task. The caretakers may not know how to express their feelings to the child because in our present culture death is no longer part of everyday life. In addition, when a family member or friend dies, the adults are immersed in their own personal grief and have little energy or emotion left to help the child. Adults may also find themselves with little support as their friends and family retreat.

Children who lose a family member to death often feel alone, different, and have no idea how to cope. They don't know who they can talk to. Sometimes children bottle up their own emotions to protect their grieving parent or caretakers.

Children have magical thinking and often get false ideas, such as if only they had been better behaved mommy would not have gotten cancer. Or their sister died because one day in anger they yelled, "I wish you were dead!" They need to be reassured that thoughts, words, and wishes do not make things happen.

When someone has cancer or another serious illness, the entire family has the illness. When someone close dies, it stays with the children for the rest of their lives. Children need help and support in this difficult time, and it is a time that their caretakers have limited emotional resources.

We recommend using this book by giving it to the child with a box of crayons or colored pencils. Young children may need a caring adult to sit by their side, to read

4

the words with them, and possibly to write the child's words on the page. Encourage them to do a page or two at a time, but of course never force them. There is always another time. It is important to give children the freedom to write or draw whatever they want. Don't give suggestions or guidance. This book is for expression, not a work of art.

The child's finished page is an opportunity for discussion. Ask them questions. Allow them to ask you questions. Answer their questions honestly and at the child's level of understanding. Be patient if the same question is asked over and over. To young children death is not a permanent concept. They might need to be patiently reminded that the loved one is not coming back. Older children who understand the permanence of death still might ask questions repeatedly. Death of a loved one is difficult for any of us to comprehend.

Some questions have no answers. Acknowledge the child's feelings. Talk about your own feelings. It is okay if your children see you upset or see you cry. They need reassurance that they are loved and are not alone in their grief. If one of the children's caretakers died, the children need reassurance that they will be cared for. They need support and as much as possible the structure of their normal life. Children may ask if you are going to die. Of course you can't give that reassurance, but you can say that you plan to live a long life and be around as long as they need you.

This is one of the hardest things you will ever do. We understand and we hope this book helps you and the grieving child in this journey.

Someone I love died.

I miss _____ very much.

(name of special person)

Draw or paste a picture of your special person.

This book is about _____

(name of loved one who died)

Written by_____

(your name)

On _____

(date)

Everyone is born, lives, and dies.
Death is the end of life.
When someone dies, they cannot come back.
Death is forever.

Some people die from cancer.
Some people die from accidents.
Some people die from diseases or old age.

Sometimes we think things we wish we had not thought.
Sometimes we say things we wish we had not said.
Nothing we say or think makes someone die.

Remember some of the
special times you had together.

1._____

2._____

3._____

Draw a picture of one of your special times.

What made this person important to you?

What did you learn from this person?

(answer these questions by writing or drawing a picture)

Pretend you can send a message to this person.
Write a message or draw a picture in the balloon.

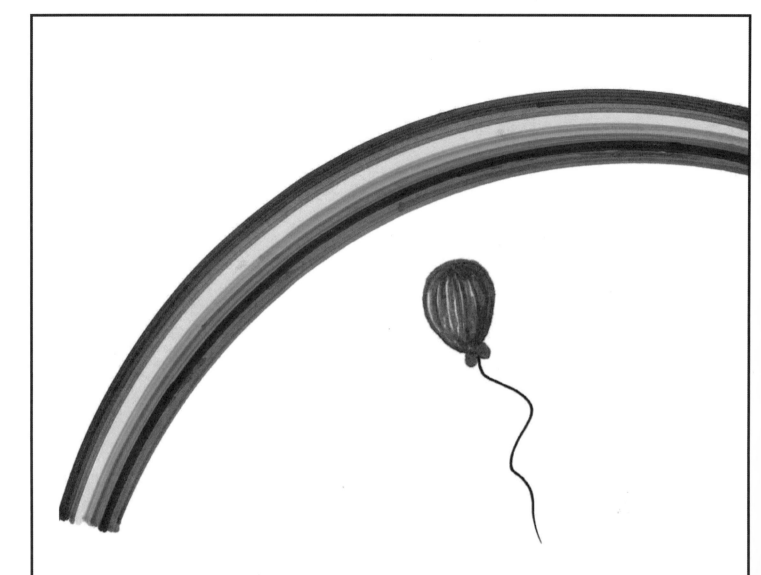

Most people think that when someone dies their spirit or soul leaves their body. The spirit of a person is not something you can see or touch. The spirit is what makes someone special.

All of this is hard to understand.

Everyone has questions when someone special dies. It is important you share your feelings and ask questions.

These are some of my questions:

1. _____

2. _____

3. _____

4. _____

5. _____

People have many feelings when someone they love dies. How you feel changes all the time.

These are some of those feelings:

 Sad

 Angry

 Lonely

 Relieved

 Afraid

 Worried

 Stomachache

 Guilty

 Empty

 Headache

 Happy

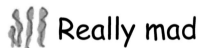 Really mad

 Scared

 Confused

 Tired

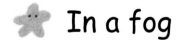 In a fog

 Better now

 Helpless

 Sorry

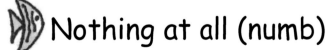 Nothing at all (numb)

I feel_____

I feel_____

I feel_____

I feel_____

I feel_____

Write some of your feelings on the lines.

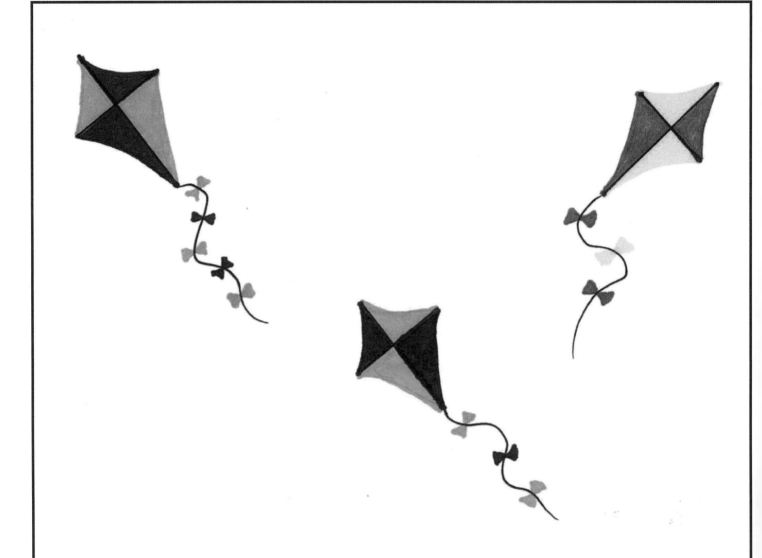

All these feelings and many others will come and go for months or even for years. It can take a very long time to accept that someone you love is gone forever.

Sometimes it seems as if life will never be the same again.

In some ways you never get over the death of someone who was important to you. Your memories and feelings will always be part of your life.

When someone you love dies you can feel very lonely. Your friends might not understand. They might not know what to say or do.

Talking to people who care about you helps.

I can talk to _____

(names of people you can talk to)

It is important to remember that people care about you. You are not alone.

People who care about me:

Family: _____

Friends: _____

Teachers, coaches, other adults: _____

_____

_____

Even though you miss someone, it is ok to have fun and feel happy.

Draw a picture of something fun you like to do.

Doing things you enjoy helps you feel better.

What makes <u>you</u> feel better?

Music

Exercise

Art projects

Playing

Dancing

Talking

Being with friends

Sports

Other things: _____

_____

_____

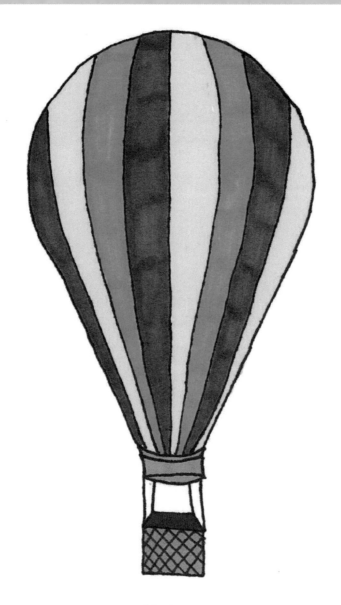

As time goes on you will have more happy times and fewer sad times. Sometimes it takes a long time to feel like life is really happy again.

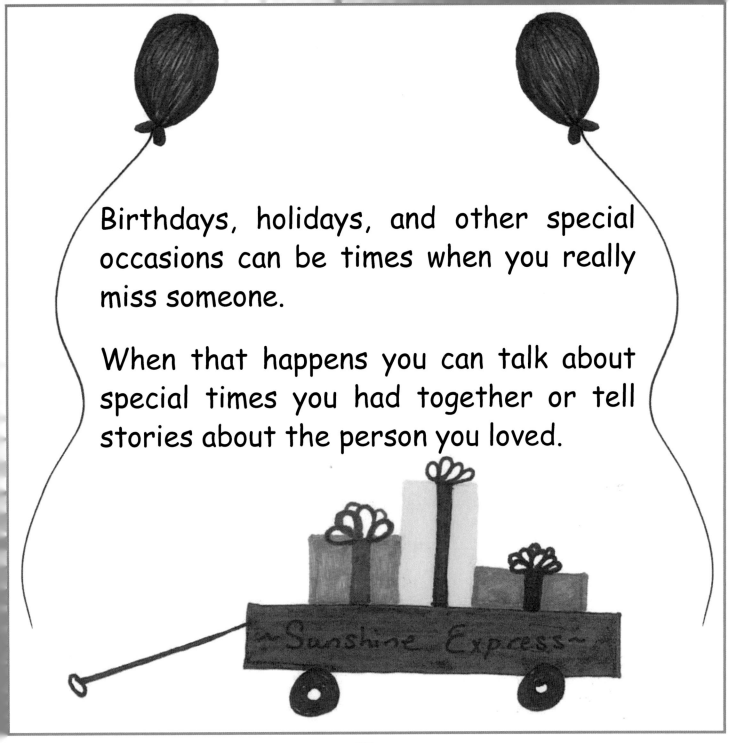

Birthdays, holidays, and other special occasions can be times when you really miss someone.

When that happens you can talk about special times you had together or tell stories about the person you loved.

You can remember your loved one in special ways.

You can:

Release a balloon

Draw a picture

Write a story

Write a letter

Put flowers in a special place

Draw a picture of how you would like to honor your special person.

Over time you can use your memories and feelings to help others. You can talk to a friend who is sad. You can tell them you understand. You can make them a card or tell them a story.

Write inside this heart thoughts or memories you want to keep close to your heart.

Memories of the person you loved will always be with you.

You can miss someone very much and still have a happy life. Your memories will always keep the person you lost close to your heart.

ABOUT THE AUTHORS

Susan E. Foley, M.D., F.A.A.P., is a board certified pediatrician who lives and works in South Florida. Involved in many non-profit organizations which serve the welfare and mental health of children and families, she served on the board of several of these organizations. Her husband died from cancer in 1998. She found few resources available to help her daughter at this difficult time, so together they wrote this book to help other children faced with the death of a loved one.

Regen Foley is a student at Tulane University. She has been involved in community service all of her life. Regen lost her beloved step-father to cancer on her tenth birthday. In his honor she founded and runs her own non-profit organization, The Sunshine Project, Inc. [a 501(c)(3)]. She survived a life threatening illness herself at the age of fifteen.